CW00798176

THE HASTINGS SERIES

Trusts and Foundations
Fundraising
Success
Top Tips

Valuable Lessons from an Old-Dog Fundraiser

Ewan Hastings MInstF (Dip)

www.positivefundraising.yolasite.com

All Rights Reserved

Copyright © 2016 Ewan Hastings

All rights reserved.

ISBN-13: 978-1533422811

ISBN-10: 1533422818

DEDICATION

To Laura, Emily and Gregor for their unstinting love and support throughout my long fundraising career and all my fellow fundraisers and managers who I have learned from, or who made me realise what I needed to do in my fundraising to make it happen.

ABOUT THE AUTHOR

Ewan Hastings has worked as a full-time fundraiser for nine UK charities, both large and small, in a fundraising career spanning over 20 years, over 15 of which have been as a trusts and foundations fundraiser. He loves passing on his fundraising knowledge, gleaned throughout his career, to help you on the road to success.

He was formerly a committee member of The Institute of Fundraising's Scottish Trusts, Foundations and Statutory Special Interest Group. He has sat on the committee, and been Chair, of the Institute of Fundraising's Scottish Corporate Special Interest Group.

Ewan has also spoken at fundraising conferences organised by The Institute of Fundraising and Professional Fundraising Magazine on various aspects of fundraising including raising funds from trusts and foundations.

He is currently the Trusts and Corporate Fundraiser for Waverley Care in Edinburgh, Scotland.

He has two grown-up children and lives with his wife just south of Edinburgh.

INTRODUCTION

If you're like many fundraisers these days, you've probably been to a few fundraising networking groups and maybe even attended a course on how to apply for funding to charitable trusts and foundations. Perhaps you've even been to a number of seminars at one of the many fundraising conferences. You probably have a few tips yourself that you think are winners. Yet, you're still having challenges with trying to know it all to keep your line manager and trustees happy and the money coming in.

This book, although small, will help you fine-tune your trust fundraising skills, build on your strengths and create more good fundraising habits. If you are new to raising funds from trusts and foundations, this book will supercharge your knowledge. Think of it as a practical manual for fundraising success, ready to take you to a higher plane of knowledge. From whichever angle you're approaching this book; you'll find it a fantastic resource to mastering the intricacies of securing funds from trusts and foundations.

In these pages is a collection of many hints and tips for everything to do with raising funds from charitable trusts and foundations that have proven effective over the years, not just for me, but for many other old-dog fundraisers out there. Each one has been condensed to make this one of the easiest and quickest books to read on trusts and foundations fundraising ever!

The more you consistently use these ideas the better they'll work for you. To help with your reading, I refer to all charitable trusts and foundations as simply "trusts" in this book.

As you look through these tips remember that you will need to follow the Institute of Fundraising's Code of Fundraising Practice if you work in the UK, or your own country's professional membership organisation for fundraising. Also, be aware of any local and national charity laws you need to follow.

I wish you all the success in your trusts and foundations fundraising as you seek to fine tune your fundraising skills. I truly wish I'd had a book like this when I started off in my fundraising career all these years ago!

Ewan Hastings MInstF(Dip)

TABLE OF CONTENTS

CHAPTER 1

GET THE BASICS RIGHT

- THE most important two tips in seeking funding from charitable trusts and foundations is to make sure that when you apply you a) read and understand the questions being asked by the trust, noting any key words and b) answer these questions <u>exactly</u>.

- The more your project fits with a particular trust's criteria, the better the chance you have of success.

- Most charities, if writing "an application" where the trust doesn't specify how long an application should be, do a one-sided cover letter introducing the funding being sought, along with a two to three page application detailing the project.

- In an ideal world 20% of trusts income should come from a host of smaller trusts you send applications out to every month, whilst 80% should come from a smaller, select group of trusts receiving very well researched and individually written applications, carefully targeted to each trust.

- It's vital to get organised in your trusts fundraising. To have a list of prospective trusts, together with a list of warm trusts that have already given to you over the years, is the starting point to good trusts fundraising. Read the important chapter on Getting Organised.

- Like all forms of fundraising, trusts fundraising is all about relationship building. Get to know trusts' correspondents and/or trustees and work with them to develop relationships and keep the funds coming in. If you build a good relationship with a correspondent they will quite often recommend your charity to another charitable trust that they administer, or another trust entirely.

CHAPTER 2

DO YOUR RESEARCH

- In the UK, most charity fundraisers do their research using the Directory of Social Change's ww.trustfunding.org. uk, a searchable website of all charitable trusts in the UK providing grants to voluntary sector groups. If you can't afford to pay the annual subscription on this, most local libraries and local voluntary organisation councils in the UK subscribe to similar service which you can access for free. Other countries have similar online resources.

- Other suggested research resources in the UK include www.fundingcentral. org.uk, www.grantfinder.co.uk, in Scotland: www.fundingscotland.com, in Wales: www.wcva.org.uk/

funding/search, in Northern Ireland: www.grant-tracker.org

- If a trust doesn't have a website, you can get valuable information on what they may fund from their latest annual accounts shown on each trust's listing on The Charity Commission website.

- If at all possible get a name of the trust's correspondent and add it to your cover letter. This shows you've done your research on the trust.

- Occasionally check to see if the correspondent is still working for the trust and if you still have the up to date address. Correct your trust records accordingly.

- Know when a trust's next application submission deadline date is, if it's not shown on their website or trust record.

- See what trusts your competitors are applying to, by looking at their annual report and accounts. Similarly, I'd recommend not listing trusts that support your own organisation in your own accounts (unless it's a condition of accepting the grant) as your competitors can see who's funding your charity.

- Always call the trust in the first instance (if there's a phone number listed) to see if your project meets their initial criteria and to ascertain if funding is still available. It also lets them find out a little more about your organisation. Rapport is very important in trust fundraising!

- Inside advice gleaned from a conversation with a trust's administrator is the key to real trusts' success. This is especially true when very large grants are sought.

- It is essential that you listen to the advice that you get from a trust and that you adapt your application to accommodate it, without compromising your goals.

- It's very useful to identify a solicitor and then network with that solicitor to try and get more funding from their client trusts.

- It's vital to do some analysis on your trust fundraising to gain valuable insights to what's successful or not. At a minimum, I would recommend calculating the ratio between successful applications to the number of applications being sent out in a year. Think about where you are getting most success i.e. is it with larger or smaller trusts, and was there a tweak or tweaks you made to an application/s that proved to be more successful?

CHAPTER 3

WRITING YOUR APPLICATION

- ALWAYS make contact with a trusts administrator/correspondent BEFORE starting to write your application to find out if funding is still available. This can save you a lot of wasted time.

- Really examine your project: Does it *really* meet a need? Are there other organisations out there doing the same thing? Ask questions about the project to your service staff. Are the statements you are making true? You must ensure they are!

- Read the eligibility criteria that trusts list and write your application referring to these criteria.

- Avoid using jargon and/or buzz words.

- Poor spelling will count against you.

- Bullet points can replace long paragraphs of text.

- Be different: can you make a bullet point out of your charity's logo or symbol?

- I like to start my applications with this sentence, which I think encapsulates everything that follows: *This is a request from (name of charity) to (name of trust) for £ (amount of money being requested) for (the purpose, simply stated).*

- Break down each question asked into its component parts and answer each of these parts in turn.

- Split your application into sections with headings such as "Summary", "Introduction to the charity", "The [name of] project", "Why we need your support" etc.

- A maximum of one to two real stories or case studies are a good way of putting over the value of a project to your reader.

- It's sometimes useful to mention what will *not* be achieved if a grant is *not* made.

- Think about the overall impression you want the reader of your application to be left with e.g. if yours is a dynamic charity, your application must, itself, be dynamic.

- If you are asked to provide evidence of who your organisation is, simply print off your charity's details from www.charitycommission.gov.uk, www.oscr.org.uk or your own country's charity regulator and enclose it.

- To rate the success of a future project think "What would success look like and what would we know when we got there?"

- Put in the differences that your project has made to the people / animals / science you support.

- Adding in a quote from a service user at the top of the application can give the application clout.

- Add in any evaluation documents done on the charity or services. They really help to enlighten a project.

- Make large funding applications easier to write: Pull out the questions from the application form and go through each question with your service colleagues, writing down their answers. (This is best done away from the office where you can concentrate on the answers they give.) Add in your "fundraiser-speak" to prompt further writing for your answers e.g. "explain that to me?", "so how does that intervention REALLY help our service users?", "and by doing that, it means…?" You'll get a far better handle on the project and write the application fairly quickly.

- It is always reassuring to a trust if an influential and respected third party endorses an application.

- Statistics: Put them in to your application, but they must be qualified.

- If a trust says "send an application letter", send them your application within the structure of a letter. Do not send them a cover letter and a separate application.

CHAPTER 4

MONEY

- Don't ask for too much money. Don't ask for too little money. If you are unsure it's always better speaking to the trust directly to find out what is the right amount.

- A good way to mention money is to write: "We are seeking a grant up to…."

- Put the amount you are asking for in the summary of your application. Mention it in your cover letter too.

- Equipping a building? Enclose a shopping list of items you need.

- If costs are broken down, be upfront with who've you approached for the other costs.

- If you think of something that might raise alarm bells with a trust, answer it head on in the application, or enclose a separate piece of paper attached to the application entitled "Explanation of...." e.g. a huge deficit or large reserves on your accounts.

- Do not ask for huge amounts of money from small trusts.

- Looking for core / unrestricted income? Talk about your services in a general way and ask for a contribution towards costs, maybe for unit cost of providing support for a day/month/year or a group session, for say 10 weeks. To come with up with the unit cost, add up all costs involved such as materials, salary, administration, travel etc. then divide by number of days, hours as appropriate.

- There are trusts who will fund core costs; others who will partially fund them. Ask trusts what their position is on core costs, if not stated.

- Financial figures – double check that they add up correctly. Discrepancies do not inspire confidence.

CHAPTER 5

REVIEWING YOUR APPLICATION

- Consider the overall visual look to the pages in your application. Are there too many large paragraphs together? Do you have some bullet points to break up the page? Have you different section headings to break up the pages?

- It's a good idea to ask someone outside your charity to read through your grant application, before it is sent, to ensure it makes sense to a reader who might not know much about your charity's work.

- In general, enclose your latest set of signed annual accounts with your application. Always print them double-sided. Do not staple them together, but use a paper clip instead, as correspondents often take copies of them for trustees' meetings.

- If full accounts are not asked for, an annual review will suffice, but mention in your cover letter that full accounts are available.

CHAPTER 6

APPLICATION EXTRAS

- You CAN write on protected PDF application forms. Use www.pdfescape.com

- In some instances a letter of support from a service user can be very powerful in endorsing your project.

- If you have a funding wish list, e-mail it to or phone a trust and ask them which suggestion they'd be most interested in funding.

- Always add in your charity's latest newsletter with your application if you have one.

- If asking for an application form by post, enclose a stamped, self-addressed envelope. The trust will be more responsive to sending one to you.

- If you are applying to a trust that is based far away from you, put in your covering letter that you would be pleased to collect them from your local airport or train station and bring them to your office, if they would be interested in visiting your charity. They may not know your town or city, so will appreciate the extra effort you're putting in.

- Some of the larger trusts might like to see a plaque on a wall of your charity acknowledging their large grant and stating what it paid for.

- If a trust has numerous rules on how to apply e.g. "send your application by post" or "send an application letter" etc., make sure you apply all the rules.

CHAPTER 7

GETTING ORGANISED FOR GOOD
TRUSTS FUNDRAISING

- Bring all your trusts records together. Start keeping a Trusts Monthly Spreadsheet. Create 12 tabs for January – December. Create your trusts spreadsheet records around the applications you must get out on any particular month of the year.

- A lot of good trusts fundraisers back up the trusts records held on their charity's database by keeping copies of previous correspondence in separate trust files in a filing cabinet. This makes it easy to flick through previous correspondence on a particular trust. You can also hand over the file to a service colleague if you need them to write a funding update on their service. (They can see what was in the application and any points that the trust needs them to report on.)

- It's a very good idea to spend some time formulating the perfect 100 word description of what your charity actually does. It'll be used time and time again in applications, where you can simply cut and paste the paragraph into the space in an application form.

- In an ideal world, you want to post your applications out ten weeks before a trust's submission deadline date. This gives the trust's correspondent time to read the application, assess it, and create any paperwork before the trustees' meeting.

- Keep a "Where is it?" document on your computer, where you can note down on which application you answered a particular question. It saves a lot of time in remembering where you have previously answered a question before.

- You must create a list of previous trust trusts and ensure that they are asked for further grants at least once a year.

- Through getting a number of trusts to fund your charity's services for three years (as quite a number do) you will start each following financial year ahead of your fund-raising target. Try and get as many three year grants as you can.

- A good way to note upcoming deadlines for writing end of grant reports etc. is to enter the dates in the calendar feature on MS Outlook or another electronic diary. Use the recurring button if you need to report at the same time of year for a number of years.

- At least once every two months review your standard application/s. Can you update anything e.g. financial figures, number of service users you now help?

- Is the spelling still correct? Does the letter need rewritten? Have you cut and pasted anything into the application to create another application and saved it like that by accident?

- Get a language glossary as a guide to refreshing your understanding of commonly used words in questions e.g. describe, analyse, compare, evaluate, explain, define, list, reflect, discuss. There are many available to download online.

- Make sure you understand what the difference is between "outputs", "outcomes" and other commonly used trust-speak by using the wonderful Jargonbuster website at www.jargonbusters.org.uk

- About 4-6 months before your grant finishes, ask the trust if they would be willing to consider a further application for continuation funding. This can be to extend the current project or for a different service.

- If you personally know a trustee of a trust get in touch with them directly to tell them that you will be submitting an application, but do tell this to the trust's correspondent too.

- I have found that trusts DO talk together, so give them a positive picture of you and your organisation e.g. send stuff out on time, be polite, don't be pushy.

- Annual grants list: Some trusts have one. Write to them and ask to be placed on theirs.

- Invite trusts to events. They may not come, but it'll be another small tick for your charity for possible future funding. If they come, then build relationships.

- Get yourself a good pen to sign letters with. It's one of these small things that instil confidence to a trust.

- It is much better to use personal approaches to ten targeted trusts, asking for fairly substantial grants, than to approach 100 trusts where you have no contact with them.

- If, in a listing, a trust says that it "only supports projects known to the Trustees" read into this that other fundraisers have spoken to the trust to get them to know their cause first before being asked to apply to them.

- Ask your charity's own trustees who they know. Create a table with a list of trusts that you want to contact along with a list of the trustees of those trusts. Give it to your own charity's trustees to look through to identify other trustees that they know.

- Do you advertise that you are seeking grants from trusts on your charity's website or social media channels? If not, why not consider starting?

- Always try and find out why you got a rejection.

- Do experiment every so often e.g. could you include a project booklet or change your application to a number of trusts to see if that increases the amount of successful applications? As ice hockey legend Wayne Gretsky said, "You miss 100 percent of the shots you never take."

CHAPTER 8

SITE VISITS

- If a trust is coming for a site visit, arrange it on a day and time that the service they are funding, or thinking of funding, is open and operating. If not, change the date. Get them to meet one of the service users. Brief the service user before the visit about the trust and what they are funding and any other relevant points.

- Ensure everyone taking part in a site visit knows what needs to be communicated to the trust and knows the answers to the sorts of questions that might be asked. Assign an overall person who will lead from your side.

- If there is any follow up information required by the trust following a site visit, get it to them very quickly.

CHAPTER 9

ACKNOWLEDGING GRANTS

- ALWAYS send an individual thank you letter to a trust if they give you a grant. Send it as quickly as you can after receiving a grant.

- If a trust gives you a form to complete to acknowledge their grant make sure you also include it with your thank you letter.

- When a grant comes in, put dates in your diary or electronic diary to remind yourself when to create and send any update reports etc. to the trust.

CHAPTER 10

KEEPING TRUSTS IN THE LOOP

- It's vital to keep communicating with trusts. An update phone call or a letter works wonders for a relationship.

- Do let trusts know if there are challenges with the project. It is far better to be alerted at an early stage to any challenges, when a trust could help e.g. by helping identify other trusts who could help with a shortfall.

- If you get any good, significant news – such as increased funding, good publicity or an achievement of a particular project do let the trust know.

AND FINALLY.......

Although there are these tips, trusts fundraising can still seem an inexact science. My best advice to you is to just feel your way with each individual trust and apply the tips accordingly.

To find out more books in The Hastings Series and download free templates to help you in your fundraising, go to www.positivefundraising.yolasite.com

On the "Downloads" page put the following into the

password protect boxes to access the free resources:

Login: Top

Password: Tips

Connect with Ewan Hastings:

Email: toptips@gmx.com

LinkedIn: https://uk.linkedin.com/in/ewanhastings

Twitter: @ScotFR

Copyright © 2016 Ewan Hastings

All Rights Reserved

For Your Notes

41167103R00025

Printed in Poland
by Amazon Fulfillment
Poland Sp. z o.o., Wrocław